D0552071

TOM FLEMING
THE ULTIMATE GUITAR TUTOR
A COMPREHENSIVE GUIDE TO LEARNING THE GUITAR
ELECTRIC/ACOUSTIC

The text paper used in this publication is a virgin fibre product that is manufactured in the UK to ISO 14001 standards. The wood fibre used is only sourced from managed forests using sustainable forestry principles. This paper is 100% recyclable.

© 2007 by Faber Music Ltd
First published in 2007 by Faber Music Ltd
3 Queen Square London WC1N 3AU
Cover by Lydia Merrills-Ashcroft
Cover image from the Science Photo Library
Page design by Susan Clarke
Photography by Keven Erickson

Printed in England by Caligraving Ltd
All rights reserved
ISBN 0-571-52765-5
EAN 978-0-571-52765-6

CD by Tom Fleming Music
tomflemingmusic.co.uk
℗ 2007 by Faber Music Ltd
© 2007 by Faber Music Ltd
All music by Tom Fleming unless otherwise stated

FABER **ff** MUSIC

Contents

Introduction

This book is intended to get you started with the business of playing probably the most versatile instrument there is: the guitar. The basics are more or less the same across the range of modern styles so whatever your musical taste, this book contains all you need to get going. Although I would always recommend that you find a good teacher, this tutor has been carefully written so that you can work though it alone, with the aid of the CD. The aim is to give you the background knowledge you'll need if you want to make use of the wealth of material around in more advanced tutor books, songbooks and guitar magazines. Learning to read guitar music (which comes in far more types than for other instruments) really isn't hard, and opens up the world of printed music.

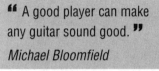

" A good player can make any guitar sound good. "
Michael Bloomfield

Which type of guitar is for me?

If you don't already own a guitar, here are some basic pointers to help you decide which type is for you.

Electric

This is probably the best bet. Electric guitars tend to be easy to play without hurting your fingers; almost any electric guitar can be used for a vast range of styles, especially when used with a versatile amplifier or effects unit to produce distortion when required. Though you may think of it as loud (and this is of course part of its appeal), the electric guitar can also be virtually silent when unplugged or used with headphones – very useful for practising late into the night.

Acoustic

('Acoustic' generally refers to the steel-strung acoustic guitar, though the classical guitar is also an acoustic instrument.)

This is still a popular, though less versatile choice for beginners. If you already gravitate towards acoustic styles, you may prefer one of these. Be warned, though, that your fingertips may take longer to toughen enough to play acoustic guitar without discomfort; also, many rock techniques (we'll look at some later in the book) will be difficult or impossible unless you switch to an electric instrument.

Classical (also called 'Spanish')

In simple terms this is a nylon-strung acoustic instrument used mainly for playing classical guitar music and related styles such as Flamenco. This used to be the most popular choice for beginners but is actually very limiting as it never sounds convincing in most modern styles; also, the neck is rather wide, so some chord shapes can be difficult for beginners with small hands. Like the acoustic, the classical guitar is unsuited to many advanced techniques. Unless you are already specifically interested in playing only classical guitar music (which is in any case outside the scope of this book), this type of instrument is best avoided.

Size

All types of guitar are available in various smaller sizes as well as the standard size. For most adults and children over about twelve, a full size guitar is the best option. Smaller instruments, while useful for younger children, tend to be of inferior quality and sound.

Equipment

The guitar

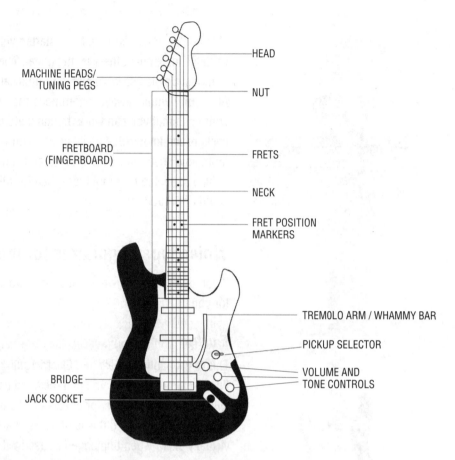

MACHINE HEADS/ TUNING PEGS

HEAD

NUT

FRETBOARD (FINGERBOARD)

FRETS

NECK

FRET POSITION MARKERS

TREMOLO ARM / WHAMMY BAR

PICKUP SELECTOR

VOLUME AND TONE CONTROLS

BRIDGE

JACK SOCKET

> " I don't use many gadgets, and I like the sound my guitar makes, anyway. "
> *Brian May*

Let's take a look at a few basic things you'll need to get started.

Amp & lead Essential for electric guitar. Amps (amplifiers) come in many sizes and power ratings, from tiny practice amps to stadium-capable stacks. A small (10–20W) practice amp is perfect for use at home or school. It's important to get used to the sound and response of an electric instrument, so only practise 'unplugged' when you have to; most practice amps have a headphone socket, in any case. It's worth spending a bit extra on a stout lead which will give better sound and last longer than a very cheap one. ✔

Plectrums (picks) Buy a handful of these, as they tend to get lost. They come in a variety of materials, sizes and thickness, which you may want to experiment with; most players use medium-gauge, medium-size nylon/plastic ones. ✔

Strings These tend to get dirty and sound dull after a while, and they occasionally break, so a replacement set is essential. You may need help from an experienced player or teacher to learn how to change them. Make sure you get the right sort for your guitar. ✔

Electronic tuner It is important to be able to tune the guitar; this is by far the best solution for beginners, and also for tuning discreetly at noisy rehearsals or gigs. ✔

Metronome This mechanical or electronic device produces a ticking sound like a loud clock, but its speed can be altered, making it a very useful aid to practising playing in time. ✔

Capo This handy device is clamped around the guitar neck in order to raise the pitch of the instrument (make everything higher). This makes it possible to change the key of a song to suit your voice. ✔

Other useful stuff Strap, guitar case, guitar stand, music stand. ✔

Posture

All guitars can be played sitting down; most can also be played standing up, by attaching a strap. You'll probably do most of your practice sitting down, but a strap can still be useful to keep the guitar in place and prevent it from slipping off your knee.

Sitting Conventionally shaped guitars automatically stay in place when played in the sitting position. Sit on a stool or chair (without arms) of ordinary height and place the guitar on your right[1] leg with the neck point to your left. The guitar's curved shape will keep it in the right place. Try to sit straight up rather than hunching over the instrument, which can lead to backache and other problems.

Standing The guitar should maintain the same position relative to your body whether you are sitting or standing. Adjust the length of the strap when standing so that the guitar touches your leg when you sit down, but the strap does not become loose. Some players prefer higher or lower playing positions but these should generally be avoided for now. In particular, standing with the guitar somewhere down by your knees (though you may think it looks cool) will result in an unnatural wrist angle, and the possibility of pain and injury.

Left hand The thumb should be placed at right angles to the neck, and should always make contact with the neck. Though some old-fashioned teachers and classical players maintain that the tip of the thumb should never stray from an imaginary horizontal line down the middle of the neck, in fact rock and jazz players often move the thumb up from this position, even occasionally wrapping it right over to fret notes. The thumb should never move below this line, however: this leads to an uncomfortable wrist position and insufficient finger strength to play properly.

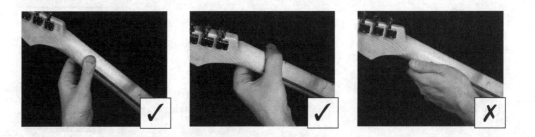

Right hand Though the guitar can be played using just the right-hand fingernails, we're going to get straight to using the plectrum, as this is central to most modern styles. Hold the plectrum between the thumb and the side of the first finger, so that the thumb and finger are at right angles. The tip of the plectrum should protrude by only a few millimetres: more than this will result in generally poor control and risk of dropping the plectrum.

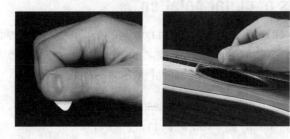

1 This book uses right-handed conventions. If you are strongly left-handed and learning to play a left-handed guitar, left becomes right and right becomes left (but up and down are unaffected!).

It should now feel reasonably natural to strum all six strings or to 'pick' them individually, i.e. strike each string with the plectrum. The left-hand fingernails must be cut as short as possible, as nails that are too long can cause pain if they come into contact with the fretboard and stop notes from sounding properly.

Tuning

It's very important to be in tune – otherwise nothing you play will sound any good. There are several ways to tune the guitar; if you find this tricky, ask your teacher or a friend to help.

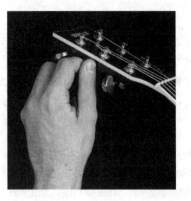

Electronic Tuner This is by far the easiest method, but you'll need to know the names of the strings of the guitar. From the thickest to the thinnest string the notes are E A D G B E. Some tuners use numbers – the thickest string is '6', the thinnest is '1'.

If the string is too low (flat), raise the pitch by turning the machine head (tuning peg) for that string anti-clockwise while picking the string until the needle/display reaches the centre 'in tune' point. If the string is too high (sharp), turn the machine head clockwise (towards you).

Reference notes If you don't have a tuner or want to develop your ear, this book includes tuning notes on CD track ❶ . Each string is played twice, from low E (thickest) to top E (thinnest). Simply play each string of your guitar while listening to the reference pitch, and turn the machine head up or down as necessary until the string is in tune. You may need to repeat the process if you're not quick enough to get it right on the first go.

If you have a piano or keyboard instrument, you can find reference notes for each string on the following keys, or as shown on the stave below[2].

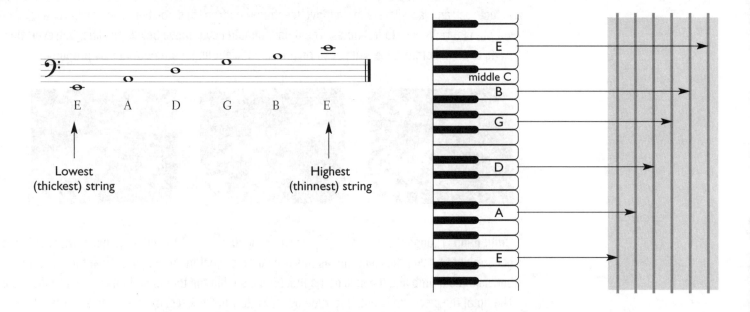

Lowest (thickest) string

Highest (thinnest) string

middle C

Types of guitar notation

This book uses several types of notation (how music is written down) to convey guitar music and technique. All of them are in common use in other guitar books, magazines, and by teachers, so it's good to be familiar with all of them.

Chord songbook This format assumes you know the song and what sort of strumming pattern to use, and simply tells you when to change chord by placing chord symbols over the relevant syllable.

| G | Gmaj[7] | C
Ci - ty girls just seem to find out   ear - ly,

| Am | C | D
 how to   o - pen doors with just a   smile._____

2 For reasons we needn't delve into, this is **not** how these notes are written for guitar.

Top line with chord symbols/boxes This format shows the song's melody and lyrics using standard musical notation, with chord symbols above the line, wherever the chord changes. Some publishers use 'chord boxes' (fingering diagrams) to represent each chord shape.

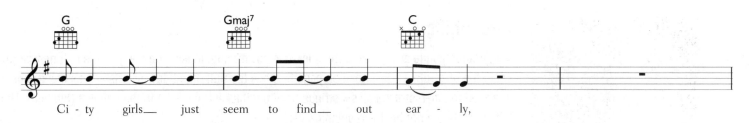

Ci - ty   girls___   just   seem   to   find___   out   ear - ly,

Standard notation for guitar Here the guitar part is written using the same basic system used for most other instruments. Reading it requires knowing where to find the notes on the guitar, as well as a general knowledge of music theory and notation in order to know when to play them (the rhythm, in other words.) Don't worry, we'll develop this knowledge as we go.

Guitar tablature ('tab') This system adds a second stave beneath the standard notation. The tab stave has six lines (one for each guitar string); numbers are placed on this stave beneath the standard notes telling the player where to find each note (for example, a '5' on the third string down means that note can be found at the fifth fret, third string).

Tablature can be used on its own, or attached to standard notation. The latter is a far more complete and useful system. We'll use tab on its own in the early parts of this book, then add standard notation to complete the picture.

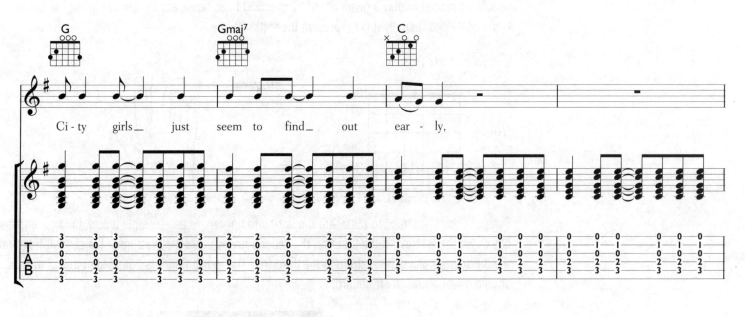

Ci - ty   girls___   just   seem   to   find___   out   ear - ly,

> **top tip** Many songbooks are published in a format known as PVG (Piano, vocal, guitar). This is actually quite useful for beginner guitarists as all the chords are shown as chord boxes.

Getting started

Strumming

The first technique any guitarist must learn is strumming. Make sure the guitar is in tune first, then using the plectrum as described on page 5, move the right hand downwards across the strings in a relaxed manner, striking all six strings from the thickest (lowest[1]) to the thinnest (highest). The left hand should not be doing anything yet.

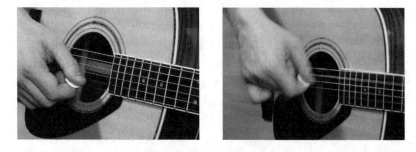

The next step is to establish a pulse by strumming in time. Begin by repeatedly counting '1, 2, 3, 4, 1, 2, 3, 4' fairly slowly. Use the second hand of a watch or clock, or a metronome set to around 60 beats per minute, to make sure you are counting in time. Now introduce the strumming as you count, strumming downwards in time with each beat.

Chords

The open strings of the guitar don't sound especially musical played on their own like this. The left hand needs to be used too, to create chords. A chord is simply the sound made by playing two or more notes at once; guitar chords can contain up to six notes (one on each string). Let's take a closer look at the chord boxes used in this book and elsewhere, which show where each finger should be placed to play a given chord. Six vertical lines represent the six strings of the guitar. Horizontal lines (usually four) represent the frets.

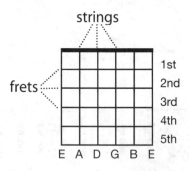

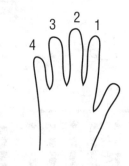

Dots or circles are used to represent the left-hand fingers. In the example below, the first finger is placed on the B string at the first fret, the second finger plays the D string at the second fret, and the third finger plays the A string at the third fret. The fourth finger is not used in this chord, but should hover above the fretboard.

1 When applied to strings and notes, 'lowest' means the lowest sounding, even though the lowest-sounding string is actually physically furthest from the ground.

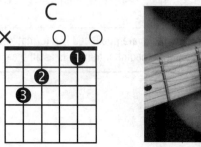

The above chord is called **C major** (usually abbreviated to 'C'). Any string that is not fretted must have either o or x above it. o means 'open string' i.e. this string must be strummed when playing the chord. x means 'do not play this string'.

Try strumming the C major chord in time with the clock. Remember not to play the bottom E string. It should sound like CD track ❷ .

We need to learn two more chords before we can start to make music: D and G.

D

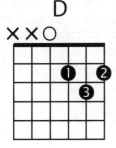 

G

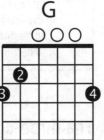 

(Note that the bottom two strings are not played in the D chord.)

> **top tip**
>
> The G chord uses fingers 2, 3 and 4. If you have trouble playing this shape, you can get by for now with this 'mini' G shape, using just the fourth finger. But do make sure it is the fourth finger – this will make it easier to switch to the full shape as soon as you can.

G

Practise strumming all three of these chords with a clock or metronome. The basic '1, 2, 3, 4' pulse can be written like this:

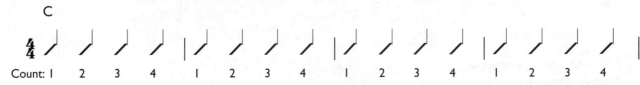

C

Count: 1 2 3 4 | 1 2 3 4 | 1 2 3 4 | 1 2 3 4

These notes are called **crotchets** or quarter notes[2]. Each group of 4 is called a **bar** or measure, separated by **bar lines**. The **time signature** $\frac{4}{4}$ means that there are four beats to each bar, and each beat is a crotchet. Each crotchet represents one downward strum. Each chord symbol means: play this chord until you see the next chord symbol.

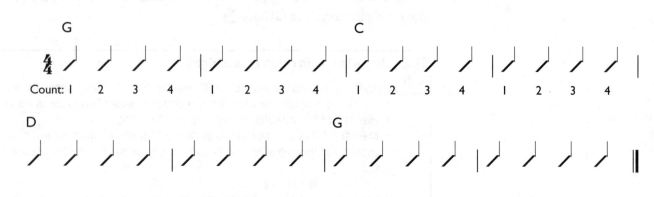

Playing this with the backing track may be difficult at this stage; you may have to pause for chord changes at first until you become more accomplished.

> **top tip** | **How much to practise**
> Practise every day if you possibly can, even if you can only manage 10 or 15 minutes. This is more productive than a long session once a week. The more often you practise changing between chords, the more familiar the shapes will become. Also, your fingertips will develop calluses so it will become less painful to play (don't worry, they're invisible!).

The three-chord trick

These three chords 'belong together' musically, being the main chords in the key of G (more of this later). Many of the most popular songs ever written can be played with just three chords.

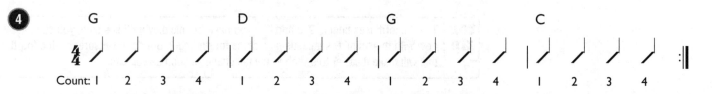

Notice the repeat symbol :‖ at the end of the line, meaning repeat back to ‖: – or in this case, the beginning.

> **fact file** | One night, Elvis Presley and his band, signed to local country label Sun Records, started fooling around with Arthur Crudup's 'That's All Right (Mama)'. When the label's owner sent the resulting disc to a local radio station, their switchboard was jammed all night with requests to hear the track again, and rock 'n' roll was born.

2 English followed by American terms are given throughout.

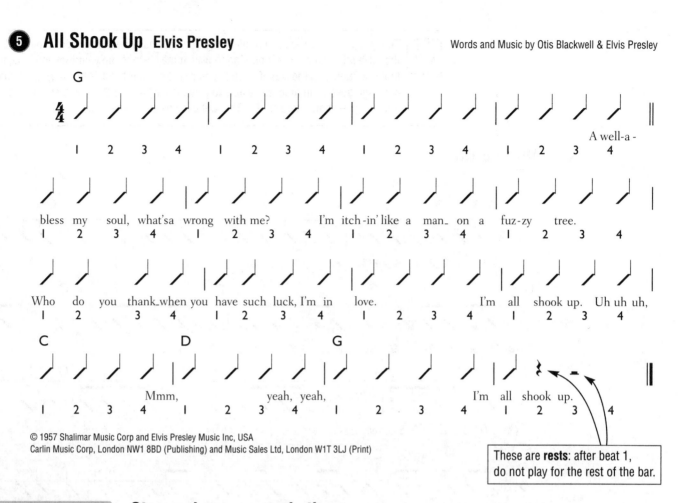

A well-a -
bless my soul, what's a wrong with me? I'm itch-in' like a man on a fuz-zy tree.
Who do you thank when you have such luck, I'm in love. I'm all shook up. Uh uh uh,
Mmm, yeah, yeah, I'm all shook up.

> These are **rests**: after beat 1, do not play for the rest of the bar.

> " Before Elvis, there was nothing. "
> *John Lennon*

Strumming – more rhythms

If you listen to just about any music you'll notice that, as well as the basic pulse ('1, 2, 3, 4') there is plenty of music going on between the beats too. Begin by counting with a clock or metronome as before. Now say 'and' between the beats: '1 and 2 and 3 and 4 and…' Each 'and' should come halfway between beats. These 'half-beats' are represented by **quavers** or eighth notes. A quaver is half the length of a crotchet, so two quavers make one crotchet.

So far, you have only needed to use **down-strokes** for strumming (↓). Allowing the plectrum to strum the strings on its way up as well is actually just as easy. These are called **up-strokes** (↑). Quaver rhythms are usually played with down-strokes for each main beat and up-strokes for the 'ands' in between. These are called **off-beats**.

Here's a quaver strumming pattern using the G chord:

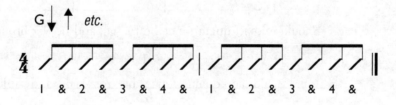

Concentrate on making this flow evenly. Now try the following, which uses simple combinations of crotchets and quavers.

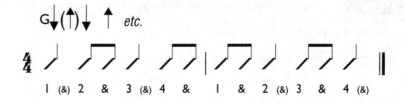

top tip The 'puppet' rule: The golden rule is that the right hand must move **down on the beat** and up on **the off-beat**, even if there is nothing to play. It may help to tap your foot and imagine that your foot is a puppet on the end of a string controlled by your hand. When playing a crotchet, the right hand still goes up in order to be able to play the next beat with a down-stroke, but simply misses the strings – shown here as (&). This will become instinctive in time.

6 Off and On

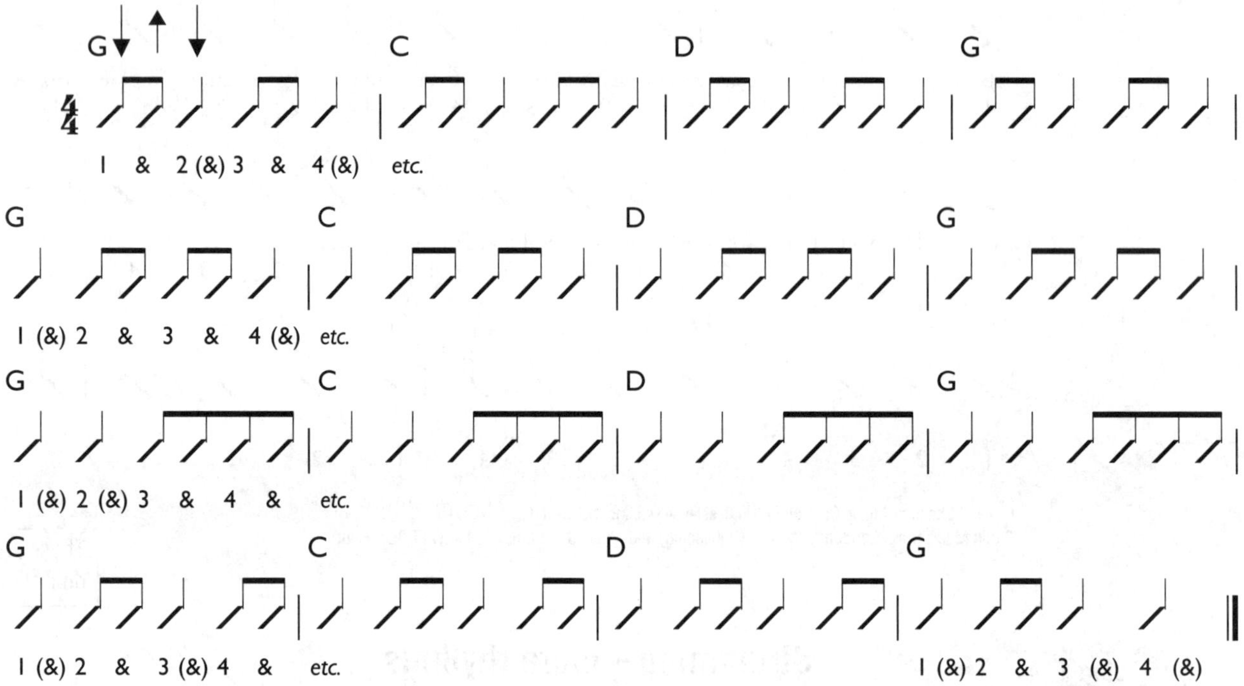

G ↓ ↑ ↓   C   D   G

$\frac{4}{4}$

1 & 2 (&) 3 & 4 (&)   etc.

G   C   D   G

1 (&) 2 & 3 & 4 (&)   etc.

G   C   D   G

1 (&) 2 (&) 3 & 4 &   etc.

G   C   D   G

1 (&) 2 & 3 (&) 4 &   etc.   1 (&) 2 & 3 (&) 4 (&)

top tip If you're still finding it hard to change chords in time, don't worry: this is perfectly normal. Only practice will improve your speed. It generally helps to think of each chord as a shape rather than separately fretted notes.

Try your ear

The following well-known songs can be played using the three chords G, C and D. See if you can work out where the chord changes should occur and write them above the appropriate syllables. The first and last chords are given.

Auld Lang Syne

| G | | | | |

Should old ac-quain-tance be for-got and ne-ver brought to mind?   Should

| | | | G   ‖

old ac-quain-tance be for-got, and Auld__Lang_ Syne?

Bobby Shafto

| G | | | |

Bob-by Shaf-to's gone to sea,_   sil-ver buc-kles on his knee._

| | | | G   ‖

He'll come back and mar-ry me,_   bon-ny Bob-by Shaf - to!

Unit 2 Introducing tablature and single notes

The basics

Now that we've learnt some chords, it's time to move on to melodic or lead playing. As we have seen on page 7, there are many ways to notate guitar music. Tablature is one of the oldest forms; it's usually combined with standard musical notation, but it can also be used to convey simple melodies and patterns on its own. The tablature stave is essentially like a chord box on its side. Each line represents a guitar string.

The numbers represent fret numbers. For example, the number 1 on the top line means: play the first fret on the top E string. The number 3 on the second line means: play the third fret on the B string.

Tablature only makes sense on its own with the addition of rhythm. Crotchets and quavers in tablature look like this:

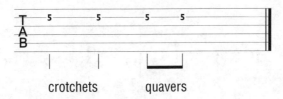

crotchets   quavers

Each of the tunes below can be played in the lowest frets – this is called **first position**. For simple melodic playing in first position, notes at the first fret are always played by the first finger; the second fret is played by the second finger, and so on: no finger numbers are given here as they are the same as the fret numbers. Remember, open strings are notated as zeros – no-left hand fingers needed! All notes are played with the plectrum (down-strokes only for now). This is a very well known tune. If you don't recognise it, you're probably doing something wrong.

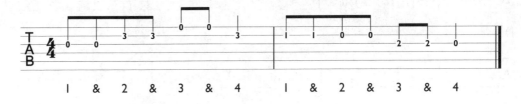

Here's another:

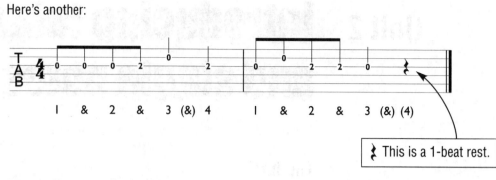

This is a 1-beat rest.

More TAB melodies

Here are some very short melodies to help you familiarise yourself with the basics of reading from the TAB stave.

Frere Jacques

Trad.

Ode to Joy

Trad.

O Come, All Ye Faithful

Trad.

5

9

13

17

Walking Bass Duet

Try playing this duet with a friend or teacher. It's a simple yet satisfying twelve-bar 'walking bass' tune. The top line (guitar 1) plays a simple blues melody; the bottom line (guitar 2) is the bass part.

 For more on the Blues, see Unit 10.

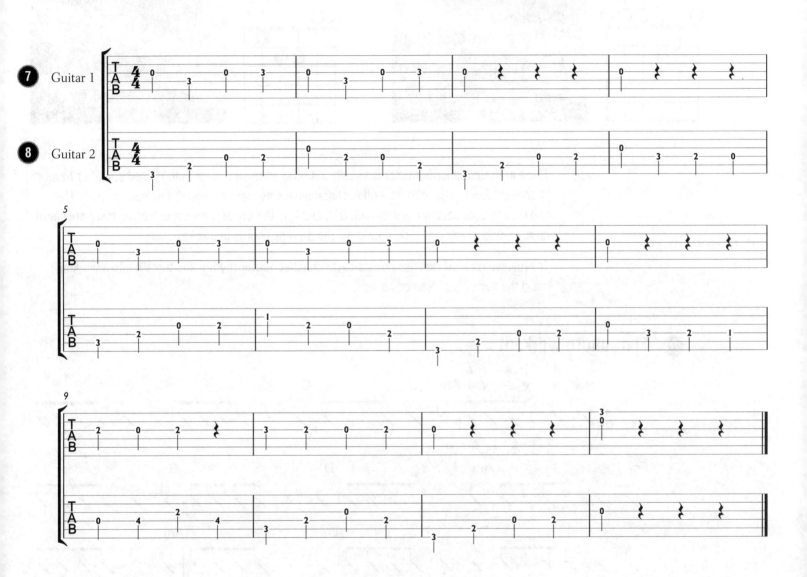

(Yes, there really are two notes together in the last bar of guitar 1. That's right, they're played together.)

recommended listening

Merle Travis – *Guitar Retrospective*

New chords and rhythms

If you're reasonably comfortable with the G, C and D chords, it's time to learn a couple of new ones.

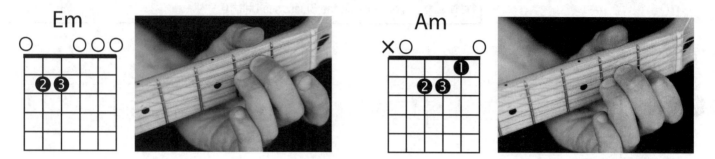

Em

Am

These are **minor** chords (minor is usually abbreviated to just 'm' or 'min'). Their sound or flavour is different from major chords – often characterised as 'happy' (major) and 'sad' (minor). These two chords both belong together with G, C and D in the key of G major; in fact, as there are seven basic chords in any key[1], you now know most of the chords in this key.

The following chord exercise takes a basic crotchet/quaver rhythm and turns it into a workout using the five chords learned so far.

9 **Five-chord workout**

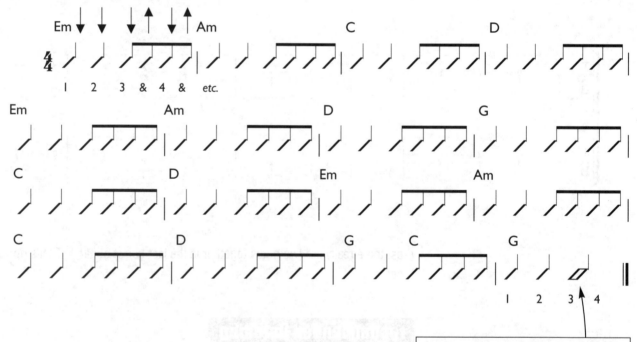

This last note is a **minim/half note**. In $\frac{4}{4}$ time, a minim lasts two beats – in this case, beats 3 and 4 of the bar.

1 The 'family' of notes and chords used to construct a piece of music.

> **"** Sometimes you want to give up the guitar, you'll hate the guitar. But if you stick with it, you're gonna be rewarded. **"**
>
> *Jimi Hendrix*

Strumming – a new rhythm

The basic up/down strumming pattern can be adapted in many ways, particularly if down-strokes are omitted as well as up-strokes. First, play this pattern:

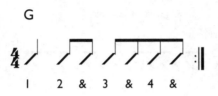

Now, keep playing this pattern but omit the strum on beat 3. The hand should still move down past the strings, in order to be able to use an up-stroke for the following off-beat (&).

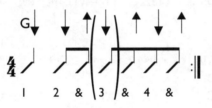

It is vitally important to the smoothness of this pattern (and many similar ones) that you always strum down on the beat and up on the off-beat: remember the hand/foot puppet idea. This rhythm is actually notated like this:

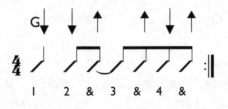

The curved line is called a **tie** and is a very useful device that adds the values of two notes together. The resulting note here is one beat long, and occurs on the off-beat. This quality is called **syncopation** and gives this rhythm its 'pop' flavour.

⑪ Stand By Me Ben E. King

Words and Music by Jerry Leiber, Mike Stoller and Ben E King

This song uses a simple repeated chord sequence throughout. The **Chord Songbook** format (see page 6) is therefore an excellent format for presenting the song. The introduction is written out in full; the rest of the song uses this strumming pattern repeatedly. The sequence uses four chords.

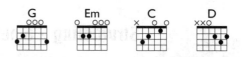

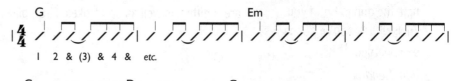

Intro

1 2 & (3) & 4 & *etc.*

When the

Verse I | G | | Em | |
night has come,_____ and the land is dark,__ and the

| C | | D | | G | | |
moon is the__ on - ly light we'll see. No I

| | | | Em | | |
won't be a - fraid, No I won't be a - fraid, just as

| C | | D | | G | | ‖
long__ as you stand,__ stand by me.__ So dar - lin', dar - lin'

Chorus I | | | | Em | | |
stand_____ by me, oh____ stand_____ by me,____ oh

| C | | D | | G | | ‖
stand,_____ stand by me, stand by me. If the

Verse 2 | | | | Em | | |
sky that we look u - pon__ should tumble and fall,____ or the

| C | | D | | G | | |
moun - tain__ should crum - ble to the sea._____ I won't

| | | | Em | | |
cry,____ I won't cry, No__ I__ won't shed a tear,____ just as

| C | | D | | G | | ‖
long__ as you stand,____ stand by me.__ And dar - lin', dar - lin'

Chorus 2 *Repeat chorus I and fade*

Dotted rhythm

Though **ties** (page 17) are often used to add the values of notes together, a simple dot placed after the note makes any note half as long again. For example, a dot placed after a crotchet makes the resulting note one and a half beats long. A dotted crotchet is often followed by a single quaver (rather than a pair); this type of grouping is a **dotted rhythm**.

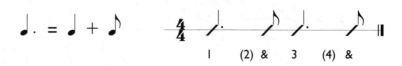

Syncopation

As we have explained, **syncopation** involves emphasizing the off-beats. To understand this and play syncopated rhythms properly, start by playing the following rhythm:

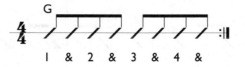

12 If we tie the off-beats to the following beats, we get this:

It's important to play the off-beats using up-strokes (↑). As with earlier strumming patterns, there is a 'phantom' down-stroke between these up-strokes.

The above pattern can be written more simply as follows:

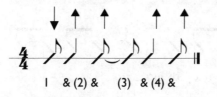

The intro to the next song uses both syncopation and dotted rhythms. The intro is a simple lead line using a syncopated rhythm and a new rest symbol: the quaver/eighth-note rest ⁊ which lasts for half a beat.

A single ♪ in TAB looks like this:

13 Brown Eyed Girl Van Morrison

Words and Music by Van Morrison

recommended listening

Van Morrison – *The Best of Van Morrison*

Review

Let's review the chords and strumming ideas learned so far with some fun pieces.

There is a new rest value here: the **minim/half-note rest** ▬ which lasts for two beats, and a new note value: the **semibreve/whole note** ○ lasts for four beats – a whole bar in $\frac{4}{4}$.

14 **Full House**

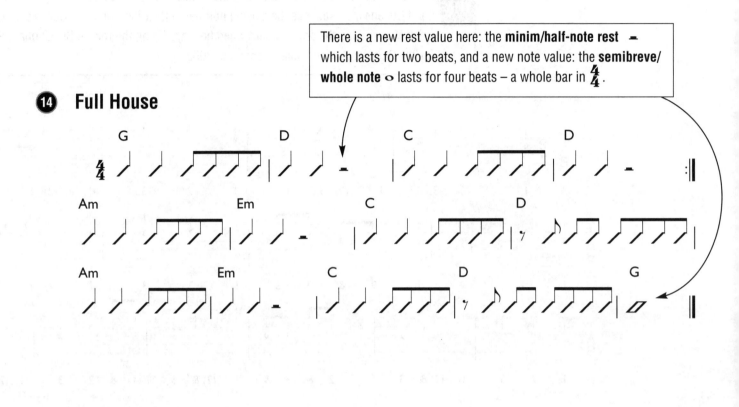

15 **Shape Shifter**

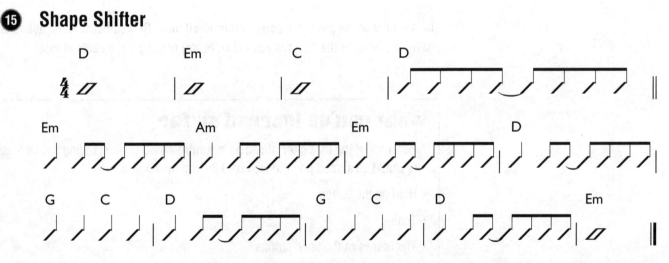

Feel free to play around with the strumming rhythms in these two pieces – the important thing is to make the guitar part work with the backing track. Just think of an idea, give it a go and see if it fits! But remember – down on the beat, up on the off-beat.

God Save The Queen

This piece is in a new time signature: **3/4**. This is just as easy as **4/4**; there are simply three crotchet beats per bar: **1**, 2, 3, **1**, 2, 3…

> **fact file** As well as being the British national anthem, this tune was popularised by the great rock band Queen who used it as the closing number at their live concerts. Queen's guitarist Brian May revived the arrangement when he played it on the roof of Buckingham Palace for the Queen's Golden Jubilee concert in 2002.

Trad.

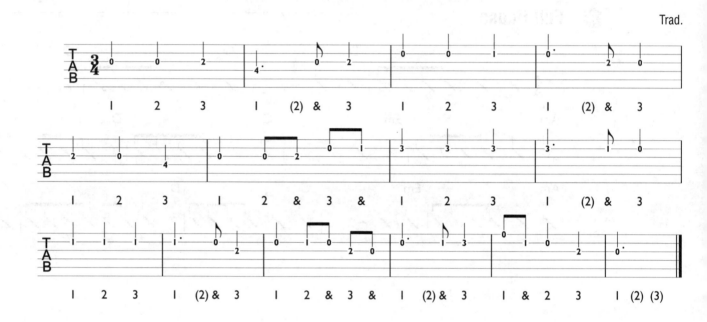

The last note of the piece is a **dotted minim/half note**. Remember that the dot adds half as much again (one beat) to the minim's value (two beats) making three beats in total. 𝅗𝅥. = 𝅗𝅥 + ♩

---

what you've learned so far

Take a look at the list below. If you have trouble doing/understanding any of these things, this would be a good point to look back before moving on.

- Holding the guitar
- Tuning
- The names of the open strings
- Strumming: down-strokes and up-strokes
- Chords: G, C, D, Em, Am
- Time signatures: **4/4** and **3/4**
- Melody/lead playing and tablature
- Note durations: ♪ ♩ 𝅗𝅥 𝅝 ♪. 𝅗𝅥. and rests
- Ties and syncopation

---

recommended listening

Queen – *A Night at the Opera*

Unit 4   Introducing standard notation

The basics

Of the many types of notation used for guitar music, standard notation is usually seen as the hardest to learn. But it's also the most useful!

Unlike tablature, standard notation uses five lines, and the spaces between the lines are used as well. Any note on the guitar can be represented using this system. All guitar notes (and all notes in Western music) are named using a repeating sequence of just seven letters of the alphabet: A, B, C, D, E, F, G.

Let's look at just a few notes to start with. Guitar music is written using the **treble clef**  – also known as the **G clef**. The 'scroll' part of this curls around the second line up, and tells us that this note is a **G**.

As G is actually the last-named note of the seven, the sequence starts again from here: GABCDEFG. These notes can actually all be found in several places on the guitar (which is one reason why reading music for the guitar is a little more complicated than other instruments), but we'll stick to first position for now. In fact, all these notes can be found in the first three frets.

This stave shows these eight notes in standard notation, then directly below in tab. This is a very common format in guitar books – we'll be using it later. (Notice that when tied to standard notation like this, the tab stave usually doesn't show rhythms as there's no point duplicating information.)

If you think about it, you already know the names of three of these notes: the open strings G, B and E. The tab melodies up to this point in the book have all been in this range, so all we're doing now is putting names to notes you have played already.

Rhythms in standard notation look the same as in the rhythm patterns seen so far, except that the note itself is round. To recap, here are the notes types learned so far:

♪ ♫ Quavers/eighth notes (½ beat singly, 1 beat in pairs)

♩ Crotchets/quarter notes (1 beat)

♩. Dotted crotchet/quarter note (1½ beats)

𝅗𝅥 Minim/half note (2 beats)

𝅗𝅥. Dotted minim/half note (3 beats)

𝅝 Semibreve/whole note (4 beats)

Every note value has a corresponding **rest.** You've already met the first two of these:

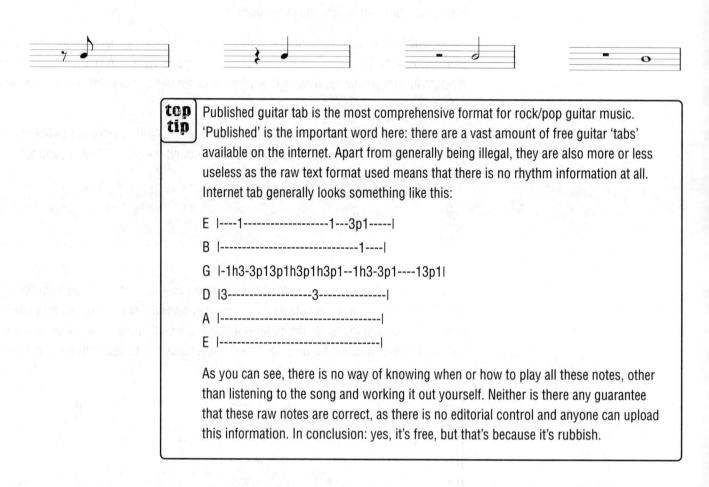

> **top tip**
>
> Published guitar tab is the most comprehensive format for rock/pop guitar music. 'Published' is the important word here: there are a vast amount of free guitar 'tabs' available on the internet. Apart from generally being illegal, they are also more or less useless as the raw text format used means that there is no rhythm information at all. Internet tab generally looks something like this:
>
> ```
> E |----1------------------1---3p1-----|
> B |------------------------------1----|
> G |-1h3-3p13p1h3p1h3p1--1h3-3p1----13p1|
> D |3------------------3---------------|
> A |----------------------------------|
> E |----------------------------------|
> ```
>
> As you can see, there is no way of knowing when or how to play all these notes, other than listening to the song and working it out yourself. Neither is there any guarantee that these raw notes are correct, as there is no editorial control and anyone can upload this information. In conclusion: yes, it's free, but that's because it's rubbish.

⑰ When the Saints Go Marching In

Trad.

Up-strokes and down-strokes in lead playing

In general, the same rules apply for lead playing as for strumming: down-strokes should be used to play notes on the beat and up-strokes should be used for off-beats. For more advanced playing styles this sometimes has to change slightly, but for now you should never depart from it. Notes on the beat are usually emphasised slightly more than off-beats, so by all means tap your foot on the beat and make sure your picking direction is synchronised with your foot – see the 'puppet rule' on page 12.

From now on we'll use standard symbols to show this where appropriate: ⊓ for down-strokes, V for up-strokes.

The following rhythm exercises are useful for developing smoothness. They are written on the open G string but any note works just as well.

Here's a little piece with both up- and down-strokes. The chords are included so you can play it as a duet with a friend or teacher.

⑱ Up, Down and Around

Unit 5   Power chords

The chords learnt so far have generally been played on five or six strings. **Power chords** are simpler chords consisting of two different notes. They have much more of a rock sound, and sound great with distortion. Power chords are neither major nor minor, so can be used in place of either chord type.

Here's the simplest power chord shape:

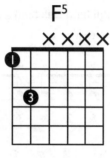
F^5

Remember to play only the fretted notes. Because there are no open strings, this power chord can easily be moved around. At the third fret we get a G^5 power chord:

G^5

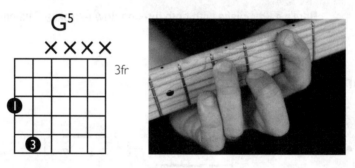

3fr

The shape can easily be moved so that its root (the note which gives the chord its name) is on the A string. (By the way, you can also 'slide' between chords rather than taking your hand off the strings.) At the first and third frets on the A string we get Bb^5 (B flat 5) and C^5.

Bb^5

C^5

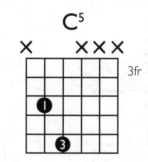

3fr

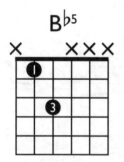

> **"** The electric guitar was vital in helping what I've achieved... where would I be without it? Playing awfully quietly, for a start. **"**
>
> *Keith Richards*

fact file

A bit about distortion

Distortion is *the* sound associated with rock, heavy rock and metal. Light distortion makes the guitar sound more powerful; crank it up and the sound can resemble a chainsaw!

Most amps have both a **gain** control and a **master volume** control. Turning the gain up produces more distortion but also increases the volume; you can reduce the master volume to compensate and stay at a reasonable volume. Or not ...

Power chords – two or three notes?

Once you've mastered these two-note power chord shapes, you can add the fourth finger, giving a three-finger shape. It's still the same power chord, but sounds a bit thicker.

The fourth finger is added at the same fret as the fifth of the chord, on the next (higher) string.

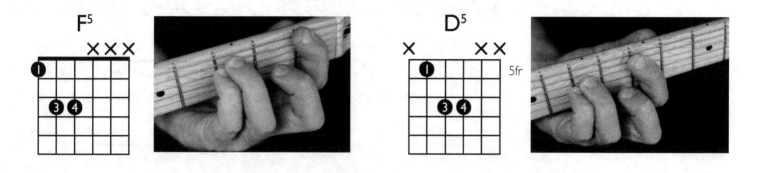

Notice the label '5fr' for the D⁵ shape here. This simply means that the box starts from the fifth fret: first fret in the box is the fifth fret on the guitar.

Power chords are usually played with down-strokes only. The following exercise uses a constant quaver 'chugging' rhythm in down-strokes. Many rock classics do exactly this.

19 Power On

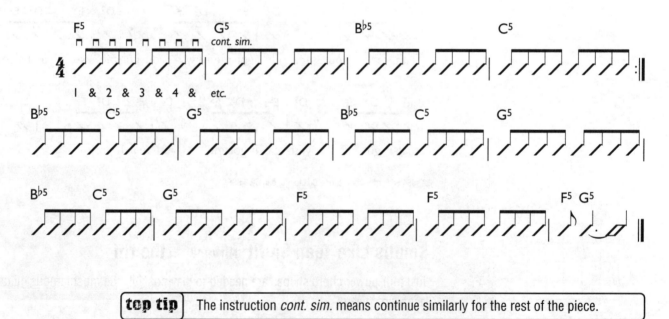

| top tip | The instruction *cont. sim.* means continue similarly for the rest of the piece. |

The next piece was a hit for The Kinks in the sixties and again for Van Halen in the seventies; the guitar part consists entirely of power chords moved around as shown above, in one of the simplest but most effective riffs ever written. Two- or three-finger shapes may be used.

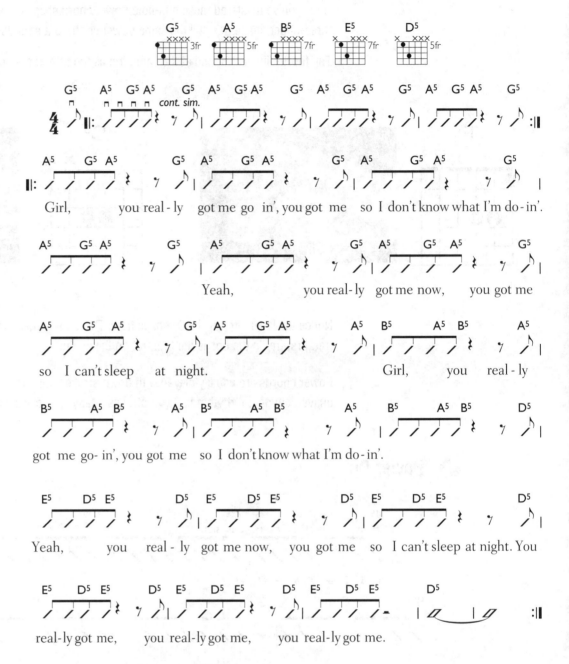

Girl, you real - ly got me go in', you got me so I don't know what I'm do - in'.

Yeah, you real - ly got me now, you got me

so I can't sleep at night. Girl, you real - ly

got me go- in', you got me so I don't know what I'm do - in'.

Yeah, you real - ly got me now, you got me so I can't sleep at night. You

real-ly got me, you real-ly got me, you real-ly got me.

Smells Like Teen Spirit Nirvana – the riff

Just four power chord shapes are needed to play possibly the most famous guitar riff/song of the last twenty years:

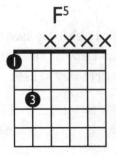

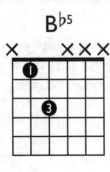

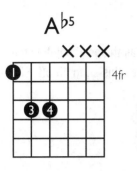 Ab5

Db5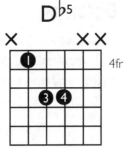

Left-hand damping

This new technique can be used to make this riff sound really authentic. Left-hand damping involves partially releasing left-hand pressure (while maintaining the chord shape) in order to produce a percussive sound rather than a ringing chord. It is shown by a crossed note-head rather than a normal note-head or slash. Don't worry if you find it tricky at this stage.

> **top tip** For more on damped chords, see page 61.

Semiquavers

To read this riff you need to understand a new note value. A **semiquaver/sixteenth note** is half as long as a quaver and therefore lasts for a quarter of a beat in $\frac{4}{4}$. Semiquavers look like this on their own ♪ but are usually beamed together in groups of four (count: '1 e and a'), or with quavers:

(21) Here's that riff:

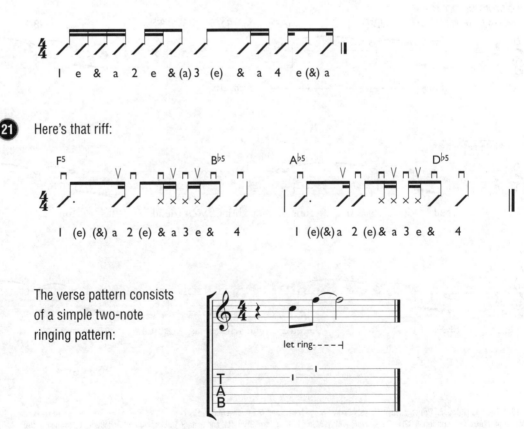

The verse pattern consists of a simple two-note ringing pattern:

These notes (C and F) are both found at the first fret (B and top E strings). The first finger covers them both at once so that the lower note rings on together with the higher note. These same two notes are played on alternate beats for the build up to the chorus ('Hello, hello').

Distortion

If you have a distortion channel on your amp, or a distortion pedal, this is absolutely the song for it. The contrast between clean and distorted sounds is what makes this song lift off. Simply stamp on the pedal where marked!

22 ## Smells Like Teen Spirit Nirvana

Words and Music by Kurt Cobain, Chris Novoselic and David Grohl

recommended listening

The Kinks – *Greatest Hits, Vol. 1*
Nirvana – *Nevermind*

Unit 6 More new chords

Two new chords open up a number of available keys and styles:

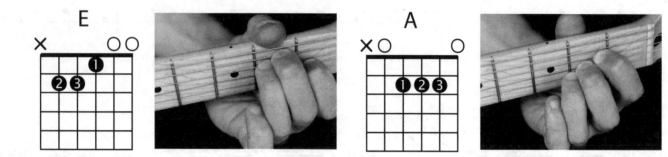

The main chords in the key of A are A, D and E. The following pieces in the key of A should help you integrate these new chords into your vocabulary.

23 Gone All Country

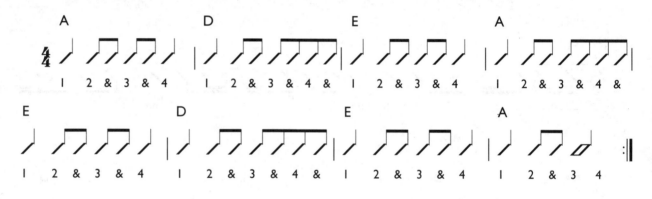

24 Funky Rock

Accents

Here's a basic rock strumming pattern, incorporating a new symbol: the **accent** mark: > .
Accented notes/chords are played louder than others. In this example, notes on the beat are
accented. This is very common in many pop/rock styles, including the next song in this book.

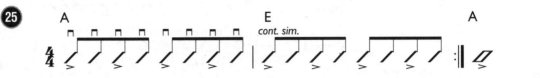

Hey Joe Jimi Hendrix

This song uses all the major chords learned so far, together with a simple single-note riff. As the
chord sequence is very repetitive we've used the chord songbook format.

Chord sequence

Remember: the ⊓ indicates down-strokes throughout. The pattern is accented > on beats 2 and
4. This is commonly referred to as the **backbeat** in rock music. It's very easy to pick up: just listen
for the snare drum and try to hit those accents at the same time.

Single note riff

This is actually fairly simple if you learn it slowly, one note at a time. It's written in standard
notation with tab. All the information you need is shown in the tab. Stick strictly to first position:
the first finger plays all notes at the first fret, the second finger plays the second fret and so on.
Simply follow the tab for each note until you've learnt the whole riff.

fact file
Jimi Hendrix is one of the biggest names in the history of rock guitar, fusing classic blues
influences with pop and elements of jazz harmony. He is remembered (among other things) as a
pioneer of the wah-wah pedal and for his use of an upside-down right-handed Fender
Stratocaster, re-strung for left-handed playing.

C   G   D   A

Intro | 4/4 // // // // | // // // // | // // // // | // // // // :||

C   G   D   A   E

Verse I | C   G | D   A
Hey   Joe,   where you goin'   with   that
| E | |
gun   in   your   hand?
| C   G | D   A |
Hey   Joe,   I   said where   you   goin'   with that
| E | |
gun   in   your   hand?
||: C   G |
I'm   goin'   down   to   shoot   my   old   lady,
| D   A |
you know I caught her messin' around with another   man.
| E | :||

Chorus I | C   G | D   A |
Hey   Joe,   I   heard you   shot your
| E | |
woman down, you shot her down to the ground.
| C   G | D   A |
Hey   Joe,   I   heard you shot your old
| E | ||
lady down, you shot her down to the ground.

E

Guitar solo ||: N.C. | | // // // // | // // // // :||
Play riff

E

Chorus 2 | *Repeat chorus I* | // ⁄⁄ | ||

recommended listening

Jimi Hendrix –
Are You Experienced

More notes

Let's look at the names and notation for the rest of the notes in first position. First, we need to understand a bit more about how the stave works.

Lines and spaces

The five lines of the stave are used, together with the spaces between them.

It's easy to remember the names of the lines:

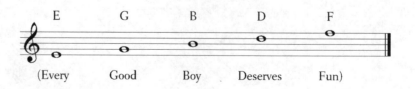

E   G   B   D   F

(Every   Good   Boy   Deserves   Fun)

...and even easier to remember the names of the spaces:

Notes are often written beyond the stave too, using temporary lines called **leger lines** (have a look back at the *Hey Joe* riff on page 33):

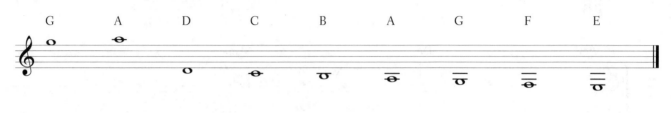

Let's pull all these notes together and find them on the guitar.

First position tunes

We can put these notes into practice with a few easy tunes. Remember, these are all in first position, so the 'one finger per fret' rule applies: the first finger plays the first fret, second finger plays the second fret, etc.

28 **Wade in the Water** Eva Cassidy

Trad.

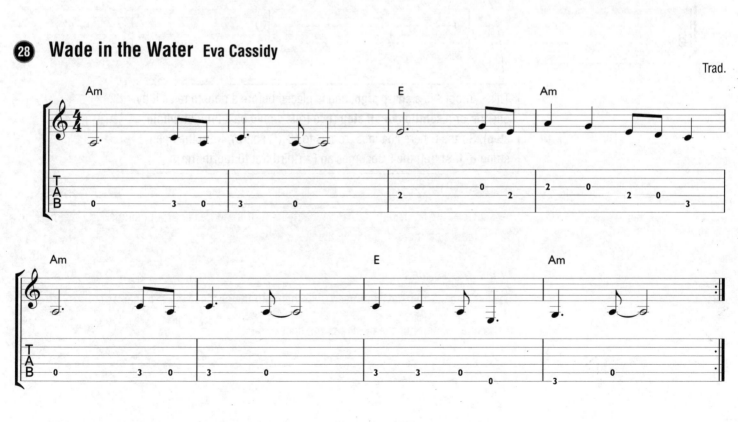

29 **Greensleeves**

Anon.

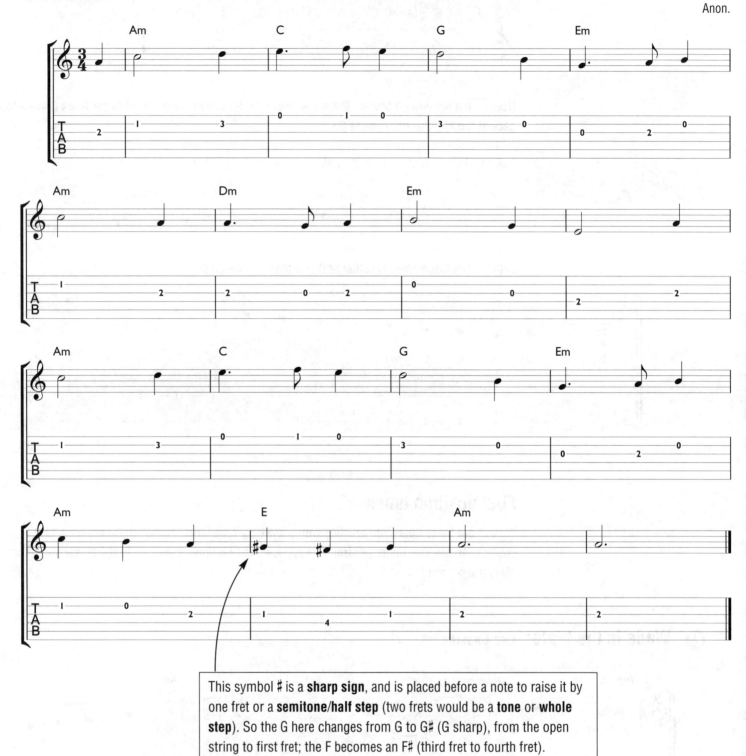

This symbol ♯ is a **sharp sign**, and is placed before a note to raise it by one fret or a **semitone/half step** (two frets would be a **tone** or **whole step**). So the G here changes from G to G♯ (G sharp), from the open string to first fret; the F becomes an F♯ (third fret to fourth fret).

Unit 7 Rhythm guitar styles

Barre chords

The chords learnt so far have all been played in the first three frets (with the exception of power chords) and involved open strings. The **capo** (page 4) opens up the possibility of playing chords further up the neck, but it's only convenient to move the capo between songs. To make the higher frets accessible without a capo, another technique is needed.

What happens if you move an E chord-shape up by one fret? Try it. Sounds a bit weird, doesn't it? That's because the fretted notes have moved, but the open strings have not, so the relationship between the notes is changed.

Now try this. Place the first finger over every string at the first fret. You must press firmly enough to hear every string ringing when strummed; this should sound exactly like placing a capo at the first fret.

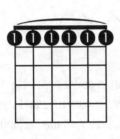

This technique is called a **barre** (pronounced 'bar'). Don't worry if you find it difficult or impossible to make every string ring at this stage: this technique takes time to perfect. The point about the barre is that you still have three fingers free. These fingers can make chord shapes relative to the first finger barre, exactly as though it were a temporary capo.

Using fingers 2, 3 and 4 to make an E shape relative to the barre results in an F chord.

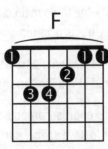

> **top tip** Here's a slightly easier F shape you can use if you find the barre shape too difficult at this stage. There's still a barre, but only across the top two strings – the bottom two strings are not played.
>
>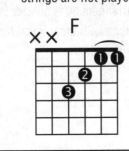
>
> Don't forget to practise the full shape too!

The beauty of barre chords is that they are fully moveable. Try sliding the whole shape up one fret – this produces an F♯ chord. Barre chords are essential for more advanced rhythm guitar playing: many chords can only be played satisfactorily as barre chords. Now try moving an Em chord-shape up one fret to give an Fm chord:

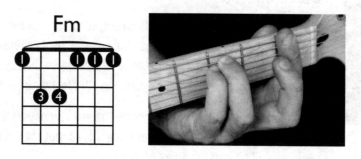

Though some styles use almost nothing but barre chords moved all over the neck, the best way to get used to them is to integrate them into sequences with basic chords. Let's try a few:

By the way, this is a common format in guitar parts. The four 'slashes' in each bar show that there are four beats, but the exact strumming pattern is up to you. Try a few, making sure you listen to what you are doing and whether it works with the backing track. Other note values, however, should generally be played as written – let the semibreves/whole notes here ring for a full bar each.

These pieces are both in the key of C – the three main chords in this key being C, F and G. The Fm (minor) chord is not strictly in the key but is a 'chromatic' chord i.e. one that adds colour.

Only the F and Fm chords have to be played with a barre, but the C and G chords can also be played with a barre (the E shape barred at the 8th/3rd frets respectively).

The next song, *Days*, uses most of the chords learned so far, including the F chord. It also uses a few new signs and symbols. In order to save space, part of the song is repeated rather than being written out again. The instruction D.S. al Coda means return to the 𝄋 sign, then play the coda. So return to the sign, play this part again until you reach 'To Coda', then skip to the last line. Watch out for the bar of $\frac{2}{4}$. This is as simple as it sounds: a bar with two beats instead of four. The pulse stays constant, so this bar is effectively a 'half-bar'.

Note: This slightly simplified arrangement is shorter than the original, and in a different key. However, if you want to play along with the original Kinks record, simply use a capo at the fifth fret and use the chords in this arrangement.

Words and Music by Ray Davies

A E D F C G Am

Intro A

$\frac{4}{4}$

Chorus

cont. sim.

Thank you for the days,

| E   D | A   D   A   E |

Those end-less days, those sa-cred days you gave me.

| A | | E   D |

I'm think-ing of the days,   I won't for -

| A   D   A   E | A   D || A   D |

- get a sin-gle day, be-lieve me.   I bless the light,___   I bless the light

| A   D   A   E | A   D | A   D |

_ that lights on you be-lieve me.___ And though you're gone,   You're with me

Verse

| A   D   A   E | A || F   C |

ev-'ry sin-gle day, be-lieve me.   Days I'll re-mem-ber all my

| G | F   C | G   F |

life,   Days when you can't see wrong from right.   You took my

| C   F | C   F   C   G | C   F |

life,   But then I knew that ve-ry soon you'd leave me,   But it's all

To Coda ⊕

| C   F | C   F   C   G | C ||

right,   Now I'm not fright-ened of this world, be-lieve me.   I wish to-day

| E | Am | E |

___   could be to - mo - row.   The night is dark,   It just brings

Chorus

| $\frac{2}{4}$ Am   G $\frac{4}{4}$ F | E || A |

sor-row an - y - way.   Thank you for the days,

| E   D | A   D   A   E | A |

Those end-less days, those sa-cred days you gave me.   I'm think-ing of the days,

D.S. ⅗ al Coda ⊕

| A | E   D | A   D   A   E | A ||

I won't for - get a sin-gle day, be-lieve me.

⊕ Coda   A

| C | E | | | | / | ||

Another barre chord shape

The next song uses a new barre chord shape, in two different places. The Am shape barred at the second fret gives us Bm; moving it up to the third fret gives us Cm:

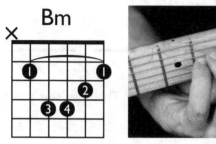

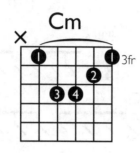

Simple 'ringy' riffs

Many songs are built around really simple ideas. Green Day's *Wake Me Up When September Ends* uses a 'ringy' three-note idea to great effect, before switching to chords for the hook and chorus.

The riff gets its strength from the fact that the same note can be found in several places. Here, the G note on the D string is played against the open G string – the same note.

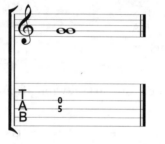

Practise playing these two G notes, together or separately, so they both sound. It's important to make sure that the side of your finger on the D string does not touch the G string and stop it ringing.

(33) In the riff below, the 'Let ring' instruction is important. Make sure all notes ring for as long as possible, *over the following notes*. The riff is simply repeated, with the bottom fretted note moving down the D string (reaching the open D).

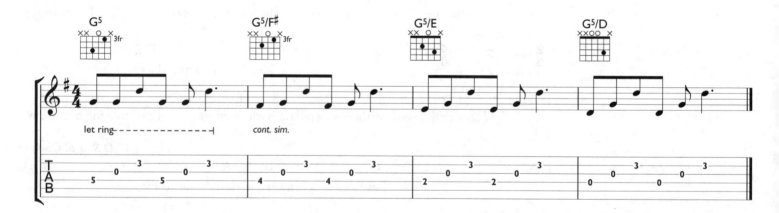

Take note of the chord symbols here – the full song arrangement is in chord songbook format, with these symbols for this riff. All other chords should be played in quavers with down-strokes only.

 top tip The second, third and fourth chords are **slash chords**. The slash / indicates that the lowest note of the shape is not the root of the chord. For example, G/D ('G over D') means a G chord with a D in the bass (bottom note).

34 **Wake Me Up When September Ends** Green Day

Words and Music by Billie Joe Armstrong, Frank E. Wright III and Michael Pritchard

G⁵   G⁵/F#   G⁵/E   G⁵/D   C

Cm   G   Em   Bm   D

Intro

G⁵

| 4/4 / / / / / ♪ ⌐ · | / / / / / ♪ ⌐ | / / / / / ♪ ⌐ · | / / / / / ♪ ⌐ · ‖

Verse

| G⁵ | G⁵/F# | G⁵/E | G⁵/D |

Sum-mer has   come and passed, the in-no-cent can ne-ver last.___

| C | Cm | G | G⁵ |

Wake me up   when Sep-tem-ber ends.

| G⁵ | G⁵/F# | G⁵/E | G⁵/D |

Like my fa-thers   come to pass,_   se-ven years has   gone so fast._

| C | Cm | G | ‖

Wake me up   when Sep-tem-ber ends.

Chorus

| Em | Bm | C | G |

Here comes the_   rain a-gain,_   fall-ing from the stars._____

| Em | Bm | C | D |

Drenched in my pain a-gain, be-com-ing who we   are._____

| G⁵ | G⁵/F# | G⁵/E | G⁵/D |

As my me-mo-ry   rests, but   ne-ver for-gets what I   lost._

| C | Cm | G | ‖

Wake me up_   when Sep-tem-ber ends.

Link

G⁵

| / / / / / ♪ ⌐ · | / / / / / ♪ ⌐ · | / / / / / ♪ ⌐ · | / / / / / ♪ ⌐ · ‖

(backing track fades)

recommended listening

Green Day – *American Idiot*

Bryan Adams – *Reckless*

The next classic song uses almost all of the chords/shapes learned so far. In fact, we need just a couple more, but they're easy shapes:

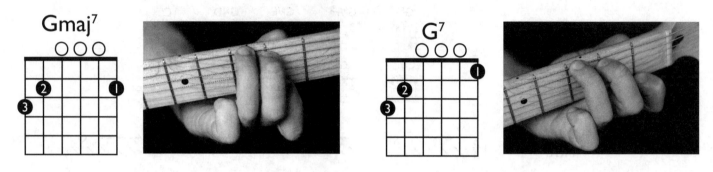

Gmaj⁷ G⁷

In *Lyin' Eyes*, both of these chords are played after a G chord, so in fact only one finger changes: remove the fourth finger from the top E string, having first placed the first finger at the first fret (G^7) or second fret (Gmaj^7)[1]

Before we move on to *Lyin' Eyes*, here's a short piece combining the Gmaj^7 and G^7 chords with some you already know.

35 I's A Lion

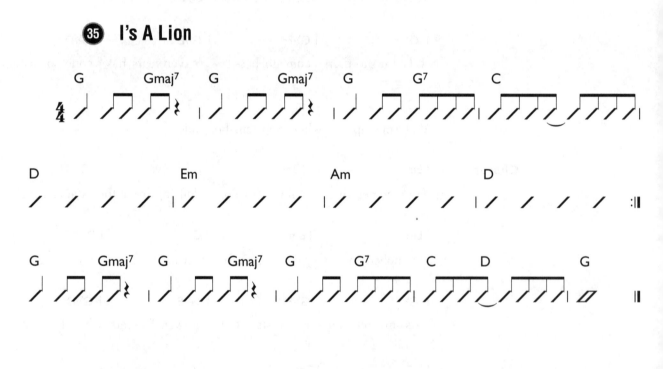

Lyin' Eyes

Strumming pattern:

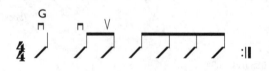

1 Pronounced 'G major seven'

36 Lyin' Eyes Eagles

Words and Music by Don Henley and Glenn Frey

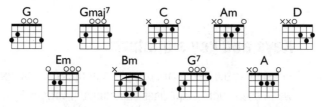

Intro | G |Gmaj⁷ | C | |Am | D | G | ||

Verse I | G | Gmaj⁷ | C | |
Ci - ty girls just seem to find out ear - ly,

| Am | C | D | |
how to o - pen doors with just a smile._____ A

| G | Gmaj⁷ | C | |
rich old man and she won't have to wor- ry;_____ she'll

| Am | C | G | |
dress up all in lace and go in style._____

| G | Gmaj⁷ | C | |
Late at night a big old house gets lone- ly,_____ I guess

| Am | C | D | |
ev' - ry form of re-fuge has it's price._____ And it

| G | Gmaj⁷ | C | |
breaks her heart to think her love is on - ly_____ gi - ven

| Am | C | G | C D |
to a man with hands as cold as ice._____ So she

| G | Gmaj⁷ | C | |
tells him she must go out for the eve - ning,_____ to

| Am | C | D | |
com-fort an old friend who's fee -lin' down._____ But

| G |Gmaj⁷ | C | |
he knows where she's go- in' as she's lea - vin';____ she is

| Am | C | G C | G ||
head-ed for the cheat-in' side of town._____ You can't

Chorus | G | C | G | |
hide_____ your ly - in' eyes,_____ and your

| Em | Bm | Am | D |
smile_____ is a thin dis - guise._____ I thought by

| G | G⁷ | C | A |
now_____ you'd re - a - lize_____ there

| Am | C | G | |
ain't no way to hide your ly - in' eyes._____

Outro | Gmaj⁷ | C | | Am | D | G | | 𝄍 ||

More advanced notation

Keys and key signatures

Put simply, the key centre of a piece of music is the note/chord which feels like 'home'. So far, we've seen chord sequences and songs in various keys. The key of C major is the simplest key to understand; however more complicated keys use **sharps** (see page 36) and **flats**. These are the opposite of sharps, *lowering* the pitch of a note by one fret, and are shown using the ♭ symbol. For example, the note A (G string, 2nd fret) becomes A♭ (A flat: G string, first fret.)

Some examples of sharps and flats:

Though these can simply be written when needed, pieces with many sharps and flats would begin to look very complex. For this reason the system of **key signatures** is used to tell us which notes in the piece will be sharps or flats. This is very useful as we can instantly tell the key of a piece by looking at its key signature.

The key signature is simply a number of sharp or flat symbols placed at the start of each line. Take this example:

The sharp symbol here is on the 'F' line and tells us that every F in the piece becomes an F♯ (F sharp) instead. It also (usually) tells us that the key of the piece is G major.

Each key has a scale with the same name associated with it. For example, the notes in the key of C major form a C major scale. The following first position scales make very useful practice.

You'll notice that the G major and F major scales here are longer than the rest – this is because scales are usually played in complete octaves[1] and these both start on low enough notes to fit two octaves into first position.

1 **Octave**: an eight-note interval between notes – an important building block of Western music.

Let's put a few of these keys together in a piece. Notice that a 'warning' is given at the end of a line if the next line introduces a new key signature – otherwise they'd be easy to overlook. In the next piece, we start in G major, move to D major, then to F major. The F major 'warning' also cancels the sharps from the key of D using **natural symbols** ♮.

37 Are You Reading Me?

Unit 9 Arpeggios

So far, we've covered various rhythm guitar styles involving strumming, and some lead guitar using single notes. In this chapter, we'll take a look at some possibilities that lie between the two.

Try this: hold down any chord. Rather than strumming the chord in one, play the notes of the shape one after the other, starting with the lowest-sounding note and working upwards. The notes of a chord played separately are known as an arpeggio.

(38) There are many possible arpeggio patterns that work well. The simplest generally start with the root note of the chord and run up and down all or some of the notes of that chord. Try these examples in the key of D, using the chords D, G and A.

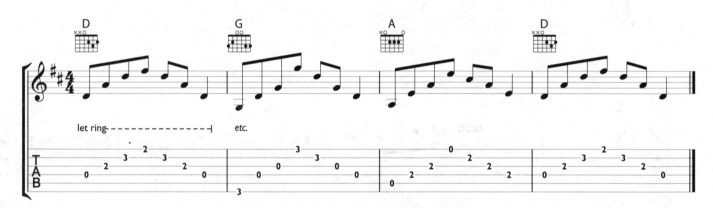

Generally speaking, the right hand should follow the rules for single-note playing: down-strokes on the beat, upstrokes on the off-beat. Many famous songs use arpeggio-based patterns, including the R.E.M. classic *Everybody Hurts*, which we will learn in this chapter. To tackle this song, it helps to understand its time signature.

Compound time

All of the pieces up to this point in the book have used simple time signatures such as $\frac{4}{4}$ and $\frac{3}{4}$. The top number shows the number of beats in each bar; the bottom number denotes the type of note used to represent one beat.

Our next song features a compound time signature: $\frac{6}{8}$. Here, each bar is divided in two different ways at the same time. There are six beats in a bar, each represented by a quaver/eighth note, but the bar is also divided into two main beats.

top tip The best way to understand compound time is to listen to songs that use it. As well as R.E.M's *Everybody Hurts*, check out *I Can't Help (Falling In Love)* by Elvis, *House Of The Rising Sun* by The Animals or Manic Street Preachers' *A Design For Life*.

Everybody Hurts R.E.M.

Words and Music by William Berry, Michael Stipe, Peter Buck and Michael Mills

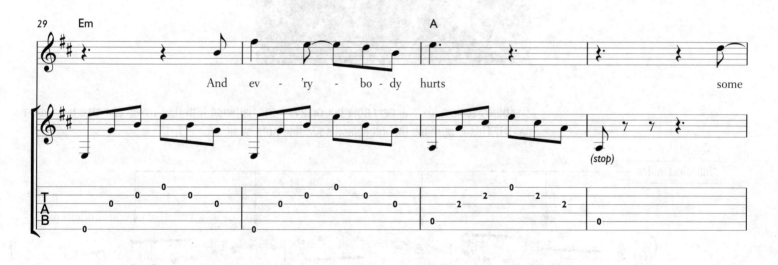

Unit 10 The blues

fact file The blues evolved from the work songs of African-American slaves.

It's time to get into some more serious lead playing. We're going to move out of first position to take a look at a couple of important scales: the minor pentatonic and its derivative, the blues scale. This scale is a little more complicated than the major scales seen so far (page 45), so it's best to get the minor pentatonic scale under your fingers first. Here's the minor pentatonic scale in G:

'III' indicates that this scale is in **third position**. This means that the first finger is at the third fret; the second, third and fourth fingers play the fourth, fifth and sixth frets respectively. So on the TAB stave, 3 = finger 1, 4 = finger 2, and so on.

The blues scale adds one new note per octave – the flattened fifth (D♭, which can also be written as C♯). This is perhaps the 'bluesiest' sounding note of all.

'Bluesiest' notes

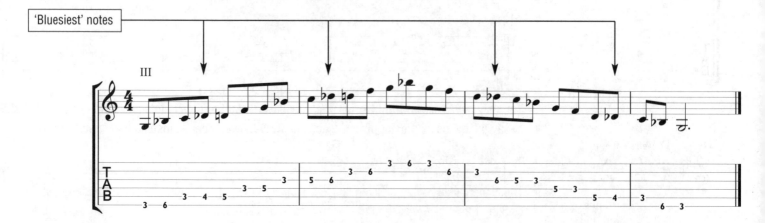

The classic twelve-bar chord sequence is central not only to the blues itself, but also to rock 'n' roll and jazz. In its simplest form, just three chords are used but these are usually of a type known as **seventh chords**, which sound richer than ordinary major chords. As well as playing the melody in the next piece, you can get used to the twelve-bar blues by playing these chords:

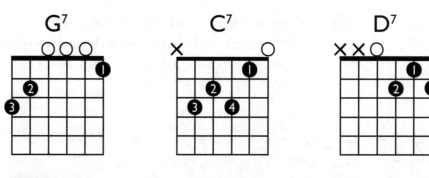

40 Blues I

Swing

You may have noticed from the CD that the quavers/eighth notes in this piece are not even – that is to say the off-beats are not placed exactly halfway between beats; instead they are played late:

1   & 2   & 3   & 4   & 1 ...

These are called 'swing' quavers and are typical of many jazz styles. Try counting along with the backing track for *Blues I* and the meaning of this will become clear.

Improvisation

Many great guitar solos don't sound as if they're written in advance. This is because they are **improvised** – created spontaneously, or 'made up' on the spot. The blues scale and the twelve-bar blues sequence fit perfectly together; nothing that you play can really sound wrong!

 Try improvising using the G minor pentatonic and blues scales with the backing track for *Blues I*. At this stage, it's fine to 'noodle' around the scales without worrying too much about the result; to help you, here are some one- and two-bar phrases ('licks') which will work anywhere in the sequence. Learn them and experiment!

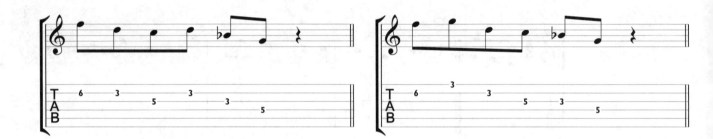

> **recommended listening**
>
> Eric Clapton – *From the Cradle*

The versatile guitarist

Lead guitar

Lead guitar players, particularly in rock music, use a handful of techniques practically all the time.

String bending

This technique is as simple as it sounds. The string is quite literally 'bent' or forced away from its natural straight course, while continuing to be fretted. You can therefore hear the sound bend. Bending is easier higher up the neck (near the mid-point of the string) so try this first bend at the ninth fret. This type of bending requires an electric guitar (or very strong fingers).

First, fret this note with the third finger:

Place the first and second fingers *behind* the fretted note (at the fifth and sixth frets) like this:

Now play the note. As it sounds, push the string upwards while maintaining finger pressure.

 You should hear the pitch of the note rise. Let's try to make this a **semitone/half-step** bend: in other words, the note should be bent up to the pitch of the note one fret higher. The first bar below shows how bends are notated in notation and tab; the second bar shows the guide pitch for this note.

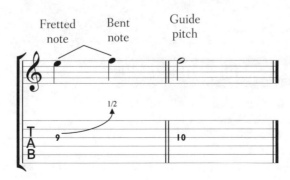

Fretted note   Bent note   Guide pitch

Slide

This is another simple and effective technique. The fretting finger slides between two notes, while maintaining finger pressure, allowing all notes along the way to sound.

In this example, the note E is played (D string, second fret); then the fretting finger slides up to the fifth fret (G). Finger pressure should be sufficient to allow the final note to ring clearly; notes along the way should be (briefly) audible too.

 Vibrato

This is Italian for 'vibrated' and generally means a rapid fluctuation in the pitch of a note – the way many opera singers sing is an extreme example. There are many ways to produce this effect on the guitar; rock vibrato usually involves moving the finger rapidly at right angles to the direction of the string, while maintaining pressure. This can be seen as a series of rapid, small string bends. Vibrato is usually written as a wavy line.

The following piece uses a little of all three techniques and is unusual in being played entirely on one string – just follow the rhythm and techniques in the top stave, and the fret numbers in the tab.

44 All In One

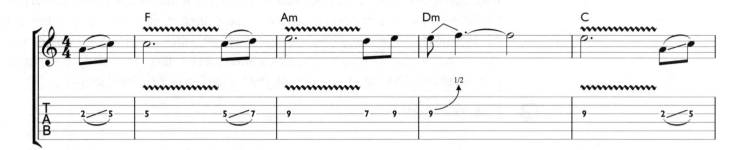

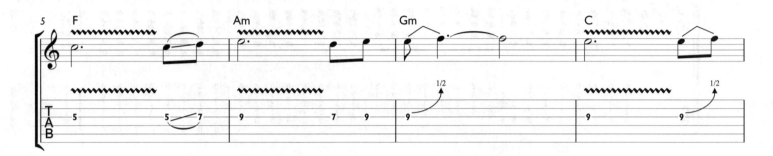

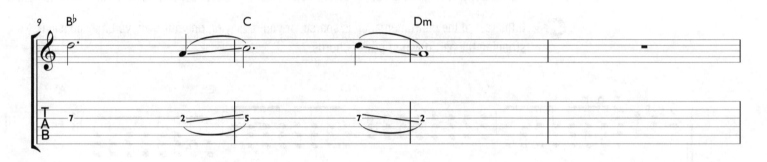

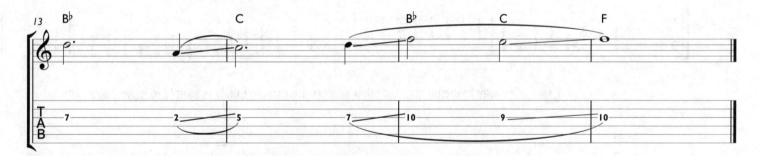

recommended listening

Pink Floyd – *Dark Side of the Moon*

Gary Moore – *Still Got the Blues*

Rhythm guitar

Many people setting out to learn the guitar harbour a wish to stand under a spotlight and play frighteningly fast solos, but most guitar players spend much of their time playing rhythm guitar in one form or another, accompanying vocals or other lead instruments. The golden rule of both acoustic and electric rhythm playing is almost always 'less is more', particularly when playing with other musicians. This can apply to both the rhythm itself and the choice of chords.

45 Consider this rock rhythm part:

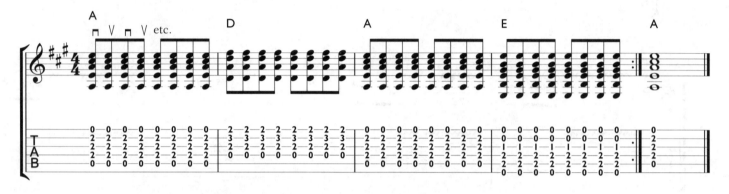

Rather busy, isn't it? This can be solved in a number of ways, depending on what else is going on.

46 If the rest of the instrumentation is sparse, or you're playing on your own, you may consider stripping the part down to power chords:

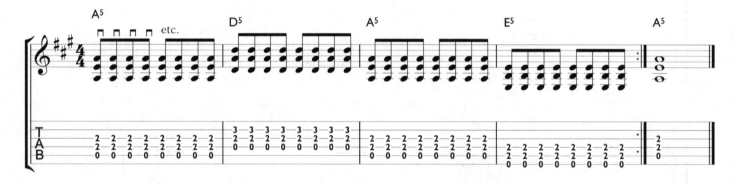

47 One way to create space if other players are playing busily is simply to leave beats out:

This is also a handy way to change the feel of a song – to create a 'breakdown' halfway through, or to create an introduction feel.

Now try these ideas out yourself over track **48** .

Unit 12 More tricks, more songs

In this final unit, we're going to explore some tricks that don't fall neatly into any other place in the book, but which will enable you to play some classic songs: some of those everyone expects you to be able to play if you lay claim to being able to play the guitar.

Lazy barres

This idea is very common in lots of rock music: take a moveable barre chord shape and move it around *without playing the full barre* – let the open top E and B strings ring instead. This produces some really complex sounding chords with long names which are actually really easy to play. Try these:

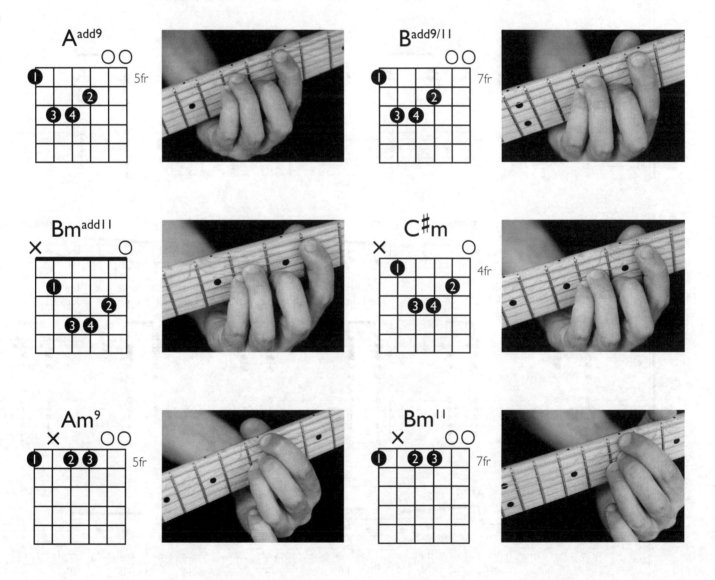

Our next song moves some of these shapes around in this way, as well as using a few simple power chord riffs – these are all written out in full in tab.

49 Teenage Dirtbag Wheatus

Words and Music by Brendan Brown

Review

We're nearly at the end of the book! If you're still with us, you've made a great start on the road to being an accomplished guitarist. While this can be a lifetime's project, the skills and knowledge covered here provide a solid foundation. Take a look down the list below; if you are unsure about any of these things, now would be an excellent time to look back through the book to brush up ...

- Tuning

- Posture

- String names

- Tablature, standard notation and chord songbook formats

- Strumming

- Chord boxes

- Note values and their rests

- Syncopation

- Repeat marks

- Ties

- Single note/lead playing

- Time signatures: $\frac{4}{4}$ $\frac{2}{4}$ $\frac{3}{4}$ $\frac{6}{8}$

- Notes on the stave in first position

- Up/down strokes and when to use them

- Power chords

- Left-hand damping

- Distortion

- Barre chords and 'lazy' barre chords

- 'Ringy' riffs

- Keys and key signatures, major scales and arpeggios

- Seventh chords

- Twelve-bar blues and the blues scale

- Bend, slide and vibrato techniques

- Rock rhythm skills

A handy glossary of all the chords we've covered in this book (plus a few we haven't!) is provided on p64.

Faith George Michael

Our final classic song uses the E-shape barre chord with added percussive effects.

As you have alreday seen from *Smells Like Teen Spirit* (page 29), adding percussive elements into a rhythm part can really help to add momentum to your playing. The easiest way to create a big percussive sound is to cover all six strings loosely with the left hand without actually fretting a chord shape. Strumming all six strings then produces a great percussive effect.

 Adding percussion to a rhythm part with barre chords is really easy too. Just ease off the left-hand finger pressure, while continuing to strum. You should get a percussive 'trrrrrr' sound without hearing any actual notes. Percussive notes are usually shown with crossed noteheads; when mixed with sounding chords, the result looks like this:

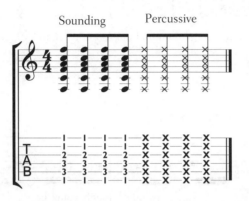

Faith uses barre chords throughout (except for the open E chord). We've seen three of them so far (at different frets) …

G#m

C#m
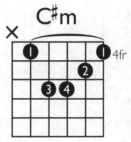

F#
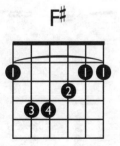

…and there's one new shape: the A shape barred at the second fret to produce a B major chord.

B
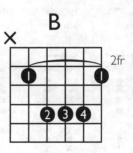
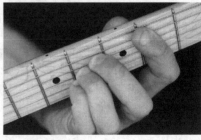

1. Well I guess it would be

nice   if I___ could touch your bo — dy,   I know not
(2) - by,   I know_ you're ask - ing me___ to stay,   Sayin' please, please,

ev - 'ry - bo — dy   has got a bo - dy like   you.___   Oh,___ but I got - ta think
please, don't go a — way,   You say I'm giv - ing you the blues.___   May - -

Chord glossary

Here's a reference chart covering all the chord shapes used in the book, plus a few handy shapes for chords you may encounter in sheet music and songbooks.

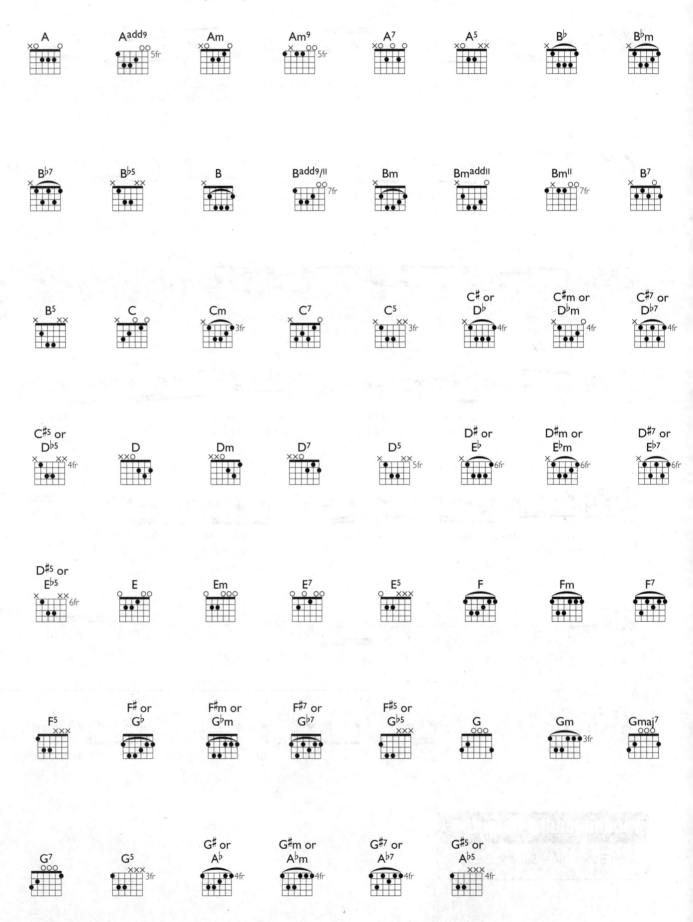